Waiting for Music

SIMON MUNDY

RENARD PRESS

RENARD PRESS LTD

Kemp House
152–160 City Road
London EC1V 2NX
United Kingdom
info@renardpress.com
020 8050 2928

www.renardpress.com

Waiting for Music first published by Renard Press Ltd in 2021

Text © Simon Mundy, 2021

Cover design by Will Dady

Printed and bound in Great Britain by Clays Ltd, Elcograf S.p.A.

MIX
Paper from
responsible sources
FSC® C018072

Paperback ISBN: 978-1-913724-43-6
e-book ISBN: 978-1-913724-57-3

9 8 7 6 5 4 3 2 1

CONTENTS

NOTES ON THE POEMS

I have been close to musicians, visual artists and dancers all my life. This century those relationships have become the main impetus for my poetry, often dictating subject, shape, voice and length. This book intersperses these substantial segments with individual unrelated poems. These notes explain the context of the sequences and movements written at the request of composers, performers, artists and choreographers.

Brahms – Poems to Accompany Op. 117–119

This sequence stems from a conversation with the pianist and composer David Owen Norris about the rhapsodies and intermezzi for solo piano written by Brahms in his late fifties. Although he never said as much, it is felt that Brahms wrote each of them as a reminiscence of a woman he had loved but never partnered. David suggested I write some short poems on a similar theme, drawing on my own life, but taking their atmosphere directly from Brahms' pieces, to be read at a recital or set to new music.

Concerto grosso – After Corelli's Op. 6, No. 4 in D Major
Every year at the auditions for the European Union Baroque
Orchestra it was the tradition for the tutors to give a concert.
As a trustee of the orchestra I was also asked to perform
when I took part in the coaching in 2012. As a poet who can-
not play an instrument, it seemed the best thing to do was to
write a piece that mirrored the rhythms and style of one of
the works the participants had been learning. The simultan-
eous voices roughly match the way the solo group interlocks
with the *tutti* group in Corelli's astonishing concerto. It was
duly performed by me and the double-bass coach, Maggie
Urqhart, in Echternach, Luxembourg.

Fantasias
As well as the rhapsodies and intermezzi, Brahms wrote
several pieces called 'Fantasia'. Mine are unrelated to
particular works (or even composers), but the freedom of
the form and its exploration of imaginings and tangential
thoughts is much the same.

Putting in to Valparaiso
In 2014 I had the chance to go to Chile for the first time. My
father was born and grew up in Valparaiso, but ran away
to sea at the age of fourteen in 1932, soon after his parents
died. He never went back, though he is commemorated on
the family memorial there. The Chilean National Library
in Santiago was incredibly welcoming, and let me spend a
morning in its writers' room examining Pablo Neruda's
manuscripts. The next day I visited his house in Valparaiso.

Some Songs

The composer Adrian Williams asked me to write some lines that could be set to short songs, as if they were taken from a Shakespeare play – like the many settings of the verses from *The Tempest*.

Scrolling...

This poem was written for *Supernova*, an internet project of the international contemporary arts network Auropolis, based in Belgrade. Every few weeks between October 2008 and October 2009 I added more segments online, and it became a poetic commentary on the year. It was performed live by me with improvised music by violinist Manja Ristic and cellist Ivana Grahovac at three venues in Belgrade in December 2009.

Llandian

A few years ago the Royal Ballet's chief choreographer, Wayne McGregor, suggested that I work with one of the company's emerging dancer–choreographers, Nathalie Harrison, to create an experimental poetry and dance piece. She asked me to write a substantial poem reflecting on the story of London as a city, from prehistoric times to the present day. It had to contain enough scenography for her to create movement, as if the words were music. In the end production time couldn't be found, so only these words remain.

Angel Match

In 2015 Cecilia McDowall was commissioned to write a short cycle called *Angel Songs*, and complained to me that nobody wrote fast poems about angels. It seemed to me that a foot-ball match between angels, fallen and unfallen, was the answer. It was given its first performance by Gillian Keith at that year's Presteigne Festival. This is followed by a longer version, *Match Report*.

Seven Poems for Blood Orange's Exhibition in Brussels

Curated by Debra Welch and Sarah Simmonds, the visual arts collective, Blood Orange, was given the bare space of an old factory belonging to the Société Mutuelle pour Artistes in Brussels for a weekend of installations on the 19th and 20th of October 2012. They asked me to select some of the works to write about.

Venetian Serenade

This was conceived as a *scena* for soprano (Clare McCaldin), dance company and small baroque orchestra, to be set by Roxanna Panufnik and played by the Orchestra of the Age of Enlightenment. It was inspired by a 16th-century picture in the National Gallery in London by Giovanni Girolamo Savoldo – of Mary Magdalene, in theory, but with the Venetian lagoon in the background. I moved the scene for-ward a couple of centuries and made it secular: a woman waiting for her lover at dusk in a small piazza, the woman narrating, all the other characters dancing. Sadly, the scene has not yet materialised.

WAITING

FOR MUSIC

BRAHMS

Poems to Accompany Op. 117–119

OP. 118, NO. 4
Intermezzo

Nothing had changed since Francesco and Chiara
Walked this way, through the bastion gate
In the southern walls and straight into the fields,
A dusty track, vines, olives, a smattering of goats.
The farmhouse a mile beyond presided over rich fields,
Tempered in our time by the tents and detritus of students.
Inside, the huge fire baked loaves in pallets on the ash,
Seared and charred haunches deep with herbs.
Latin boys longed for you and, dumbstruck,
Threw wine across the tabletops in libation,
Demanding the attention of their instant goddess.
How funny, I thought, you'd never succumb to that.
I slept alone, close but zipped against you, the last
Of those well-meant tense days and squandered nights.

OP. 118, NO. 2
Intermezzo

Maybe all the evidence is wrong –
This is the one true intermezzo,
A passage between two points, neither

One of which can be confirmed.
Business has masked a twitch of pleasure.
Pleasure, unlikely now, might still gestate.
If I for once do not retreat; if
Your misgiving operates and finds
The tumour of a great mistake,
This cadence may lie unresolved…

OP. 117, NO. 2
Intermezzo

So many forms of exile, voluntary,
Inescapable, pointless, following sentiment.
There were roots to unearth,
Nurture in new gardens.
Our little exiles chose exile for themselves,
Are fortified by beams and plantations,
By walls of books and local obligations,
Vigilante societies of goodwill and contribution
That define us for no reason we ever chose.
Every home exiles us from each other.

OP. 118, NO. 3
Ballade

Inconclusive winter in a brown town,
A room devoid of suggestion, hope or artifice,
The ochre carpet swirls twinned
With stain whorls on the high, damp ceiling.
We could not dream of triumph when only

Two bars glowered half-heartedly from the corner.
We needed comfort, a protest
Against the pain and commonplace,
My high point, your low, but each time
Eyes catch or just avoid I wonder
If those hours are quite forgotten.

OP. 119, NO. 1
Intermezzo

In the morning, bright and spring warm,
Late enough for weekend boats to be puttering,
I pushed the door ajar before risking the kitchen.
You slept still, safe, so undisturbed,
Back turned, careless of uninvited entrances.
Fear was home by nightfall, black canals
Impersonal, their trade ageless, always
The answer to indecision. You survived
And found the ocean. Perhaps I did not.

OP. 118, NO. 6
Intermezzo

Buffoon echoes through the years, so true,
Surviving pointless death, verified
By your successors, the curse of every piece
I write to clear my name, chisel yours
In wanton music, furious regret.
Our ages would be little different now,
Circumstances not so strange.

Within an orbit of the sun life
Could have been yours, these songs cut
Short as the buffoon was tamed.

OP. 117, NO. 1
Intermezzo

So early in childhood, barely six,
The first familiar ache, the fantasy,
The brink of tears, a name to chant,
And now just that, calm brown hair,
Your sister too, an expedition, silent,
Up the steep path that led us to the garden.

OP. 117, NO. 3
Intermezzo

So few of our returns have been happy –
The same little attempts bouncing off decades,
Ricocheting through generations, a hard ball
Returned by elastic with venom and a hint of malice.
Provocation was rarely a successful defence
As I groped to deal with that loping serve,
Found a spot so soft and sweet to plant the shot.
The match was constantly abandoned, retired hurt.
I never understood your scoring system
Or why you let me win a game or two,
Suggested another round, then called foul.
Once the umpire intervened – early, much too early.
Did that spoil it all for ever?

OP. 118, NO. 5
Romance

The illusion says we came so close,
That on many days in many years
I could have taken charge,
Taken your decision in both my hands.
From all of those only four days linger,
Prod memory into real regret.
The Thames hosts two; one midsummer
On the water when a pleasure boat
So nearly was just that, the other touching,
Leaning on the embankment wall
As the tide rose with our resolution
Almost to the top. By the time we kissed
Two later days we were grounded on the ebb.

OP. 119, NO. 4
Rhapsody

Genius loved you sometimes as you smoked
At the breakfast table or laid out
The sheets of music for correction.
You left them all as the shy intensity,
The glaring, the yearning, the declarations,
Repeated a pattern, made each barren.
In the end only a mediocrity made you conceive,
Genius bowed and left the room to recall
Scenes from youth, of eyes that offered
No relief, a form that ruled
Perspective, provoked counterpoint.

OP. 119, NO. 3
Intermezzo

My own bed cheated me,
Though I cheated it in turn.
I wanted to come home
To find the bed unmade,
Your closest clothes strewn
About the sheets but lonely,
Pleading that I abandon
Any contract and return.

The bed had found
Your lustier friends unconstrained,
Who, though they felt
Nothing for your art,
Nor matching stars,
Could occupy my room,
Wrap your heart
In moral rope and, grinning,
Watch me fume.

OP. 119, NO. 2
Intermezzo

We must have met again one summer, I suppose,
Schooldays over, parents spread in all directions.
Gradual or sudden, I knew by early winter
Old preoccupations were being dismantled.

Consign me north, I prayed; then, when you did,
Was horrified. Friendship can be such a cruel word.
I braved my face, was genial, joined in,
Feigned contentment and became a punisher myself.

OP. 118, NO. 1
Intermezzo

At the latter end of love,
When the jabs, stiletto slights,
Strychnine kisses take their toll,
And over the road the light
Blazes on dilettante cuckolding,
After weeping in olive groves,
Keeping masochistic vigil
After nightly vigil, silence
Is welcome. No, it is only
The space between missiles.

CONCERTO GROSSO

After Corelli's Op. 6, No. 4 in D Major
Adagio – Allegro, Adagio, Vivace, Allegro

ADAGIO – ALLEGRO

Voice One | Voice Two

(*adagio*)

Now why?

               Why now

Listen to our

       Cry. Cry?

(*allegro*)

We bring you sunlight skittering

               We bring you sunlight, skittering

Across Venetian water, breaking   Dancers with rosé

Roman fountains, across Venetian Champagne,

Water, breaking Roman fountains

Into shards of liquid gold, splashing Grabbing the waists of

               Lovers we only met today,

High silver dancers with rosé Played hard

       Champagne.

To show them joy, quickened with
                    Our fingers,

                                        To show them joy

        Drew them towards us until our
Pulses conversed with only the tip
        Of gesture, the dip and shake   Only the tip of gesture
                That pulls repeats, insists,
                        Dares us to cascade.   Repeats, dares us to cascade.

ADAGIO

        Listen to the bells, the way the ringer
        Catches the rope as it falls through the ceiling,
        Catches, tugs and throws the release,
        Letting our note strike, hold on through the ringing
        Metal and then fade away until, until, until…

        Shall we repeat, or shall we just part,
        Cadence into silence or pause and live anew?

VIVACE

            Voice One | Voice Two

    If we dance what trouble
                Will it bring?

                            If we dance

    It will bring fresh trouble;

                            We can prepare, we can explain

Take our places, relish the magic,
                    The danger,
                                    The magic of the danger
                The changes
        Our dance will bring   Our dance will bring.

ALLEGRO

Taking hands, not quite at random,
    The electric force only a first touch,   Taking hands
Imagined, half sought, but not expected,   The electric force
Dynamites serenity. These sober stones,
            These sensible streets permitting   First touch
                    Minor pleasures,   Sober stones

                                    Reel back, open fissures
                                    Tear apart their Sabbath clothes

And every particle is ravished,

                                    Banished

            Thrown between the hills
                    Then gathered

                                    In our arms
            And welcomed once,   And finally
        Welcomed once again.   Welcomed once again.

FANTASIAS

I

In these days of hope and indecision
I clutch at details, the tearing of a nail,
A new curl of hair, gold woven sandals
Letting loose one long toe, the moment
That cap rises so I can catch a basalt eye.
I delight in contrasts, constant vigilance
Versus lazy invitations, crystal against
Marshmallow bulk, too few years oppose too many.
Even then vital pieces elude me,
Not a scent escapes the blackout, no berry
Prays to be tasted or doorway prised open.
I do not know whether the valley has sweet water,
Its primal forest or its earth laid bare,
Weeping like the flat land we pass through.
Instead a cloud of average birds
Enliven a tawdry landscape, and I call
For the mind to sleep and let the body sing.

II

The Man and His Thought – Rodin

Almost awake, stretching behind against the cloud,
The duvet, the wall of marble, the breaking wave,
Your eyes still closed and face turned down,
Away from the rising sun, consciousness of me.
I too reach, push my arms back, limiting
The first touch, the urge to engage my hands
Before their time. We resist the air,
Always hold back in refusal or respect.
From here, though, distance allows a tiny invasion.
You are in my city and I in yours;
Our closest points pierce the thwarting sea
Until I can brush the tip of your hard coast.

III

Constellation – Rodin

At last that curtain is thrown back
After all the entreaties, the philosophy,
Simple desire uncamouflaged in artistry.
Your stem gains strength as it grows;
Flimsy deception, elegant wires,
Between them such delectable crescents.

IV

Years ago (but not so many) I saw a girl like you
Rise from the waves towards a Greek island.
She glistened, of course, and spoke your language,
The laughter playful, the tears falling
From her hair back into the sea.

When you lie with me and bless the wine,
Count the stars and shiver as I trace
The rivulets of wasted time across your flank,
Reach out, caress, remind me always.

V

Across the world you lie awake,
Cry and wait for morning. For me
A morning is already old,
Its fears and promise spent.

Perhaps I shall travel west and south, or east
And find you. Perhaps I shall not.
Whichever one I choose, more tears
Will fill those conscious nights.

VI

In clear, cold skies I dream
Of heat, the drip of body against thin cloth,
Banana leaves instead of naked trees,
Trying to hide their identity in the chill spring.
In Jamaica memory collapses.
In that distant and indecent forest, leaning
Down to the sea you will shake off
Your proper upbringing, slough the sober north.
Urgency cannot be contemplated.
You will languish damply,
Too hot to tolerate my arms
But amenable to iced fingers tracing
Rivers of relief from neck to leg.
There I will taste the salt, be your ancient solace,
Cocktail hope, sandcastle against the future.

VII

The scent of sweet almonds, basalt hair,
Bohemian chaos outside, fastidious convention beneath
Shrugging off the rain. I will retrieve your rejection
From the shredder, paste the words back
In a new order that omits doubt,
Tense misgiving, rout and that acid stare.
This fantasy has some stories in it yet.

VIII

Ah, my string sextet, assembled,
Rehearsed but never performed.
A problematic ensemble,
Difficult to write for,
To please (very rarely)
Three violins, viola, two cellos
Who usually refuse to play together
Or (except viola and first cello) at all for me.
The cellos began, though one refused to follow
The theme with variations, waiting instead
For a violinist of her own.
Such a shame, for when I heard her
In the distance she had a beauty
Of tone and line that older siren
Could not match, however astonishing,
Vibrant her attack.
The viola showed promise and, as violas do,
Something in between.
A lovely song emerged for a while,
Before falling back into the cellos.
The first violin, so brilliant, so untamed,
Just broke my heart and sense. The second –
The only blonde – didn't stay
Long enough to pick up the right end of the stick.
The third stayed but made it clear this ensemble
Would never exercise her bow.

PUTTING IN TO VALPARAISO

I

Neruda was forty years dead when I dropped by,
His house full of disturbance: reverend strangers.

From an even higher vantage point,
Further along the road that winds across the crest of the city,

I gaze out across the bay.
Sounds rise. A man hammers, another plays

The guitar badly, a third the drums – worse;
Only the barking dogs have any passion.

II

My father was thirty years dead when I arrived,
His city still shambolic, hiding its secrets,

Its tatty shame behind cheerful paint,
Preposterous graffiti. One push would bring it all down.

There are new fashions in town, fancy chefs
Behind tin walls. The napkins are laid

Crisp and white on glass-topped tables, food shrouds
Setting standards to embarrass the fractured streets.

III

My grandfather was eighty years dead when I passed through;
The town he knew was thirsty to equal empires

Get over its Panama Canal debacle. From him
The word British came with a strut, slightly belligerent;

From me, with mild apology,
For having just one language.

I think of him, I think my father thought of him,
As the upholder, the man of standards,

A genuflector to order and exactitude. Sniff. How little
He would have rated poet me or Bertie the jolly King.

IV

I was in my sixtieth year when I put in to Valparaiso.
My son shrugged and can speak, in Spanish, for himself.

I am alive, I assume, but procrastinate to visit
Monuments to dead relatives in the summer heat.

It is a relief to find the women are prettier than my aunts,
The wine is a joy, the hills an eccentric trial of my bad ankle.

Valparaiso should be instantly my southern home. Not yet.
No house, no love, no money and, for now, the ghosts reject me.

FOUR ITALIAN REFLECTIONS

I
One Girl From Verona

Careless in the dripping twilight,
The restless fog of autumn in the Veneto,
Modern Capulets bear down upon the streets
Armed with the bravado of a Sunday affair,
Sidle into the arena, risking humiliation
With a snatch or two of imaginary Verdi,
Gladiators for their girls, for the moment
Unafraid of ancient laws or infidelities,
Anxious for nothing, inevitably proud.
Among these Mercutios one girl from Verona,
Anticipated, promised for the evening,
Brought triumph to the new soliloquy.

II
Poggibonsi

It simply had not occurred to me
That I should pass this way almost to the day.
Love has changed from fair to dark,
But little else in thirty years: not age, not regret,
Not hopelessness. Once again I look up
From this unprepossessing railway track and mourn.

Again the towers of San Gimignano mock
Such aspiration, such small achievement,
A ruin in a dusty autumn olive grove,
This perpetual ache that, like my buggered ankle,
I can never wholly ignore.
There was a tunnel to concentrate my thoughts
Before Siena and back, to conjure you –
Somehow this time persuade the gods
To change the ending. They, and you, declined.

III

San Gimignano

I have been searching for a poem I wrote
In San Gimignano thirty years ago.
There is nothing in the files, though, no scrap
Or sketch or copy typed on thin carbon paper.
Perhaps I never wrote it, after all,
Just sat despondent in that olive grove
Outside the walls, moping over love
Not lost because it was never found,
Seething after she had so pointedly
Screwed nightly the man across the road.
I had taken umbrage to Tuscany. Reflection
Hardly helped. Afterwards I leaped
Lemming-like into bad idea after absurd.
I'm sure I wrote that poem, though;
Maybe it hides in a forgotten book like this,
A chronicle of searches, abandoned chides,
Waiting for affectionate excavation.

IV

A Voyage to Elba

By Monday, at my request, you will have travelled
On every form of carriage, crossed mountains,
Traversed the sea, trundled on rails
Through landscape almost as dilapidated
As your distracted companion.
This is all new territory, the rocky shore,
The assignment, the exile island.
You could belong here easily,
Claim the hint of olive lingering in the skin pores
Came from fields we passed through,
Pretend the length of hair and leg made you Etruscan.
Will the voyage back retain this calm,
Or shall we whip up a southern tempest,
Bring Bacchic songs to this unruly coast?

SOME SONGS

I

The brook is swollen with unrelenting rain,
Love's chatter tumbling from the hillside,
Impatient to leave me for the sea.
Wait. There is so much I have to say.

II

In the field wild flowers are rampant,
Too many to list, too undressed for vases,
They are mature enough to pick.
No point. They will never behave indoors.

III

She has rushed so far away today
I have nothing left. My dream says
We have lain here all morning.
Black hair laid out in tapestry,
Daring angels to stop the day.

IV

This is a mad song. I stamp,
Rend my clothes and yell obscenities
At the moon. She's nowhere near
To watch. I'll rant myself to sleep.

V

Nothing compares to the joy of return,
Not first sight, not riotous celebration.
The handle has turned, the door opened.
That hug. Now we will have champagne.

SCROLLING...

To where the water laps at the end,
Down in the mind's harbour,
Our berth and rebirth place,
The lines straining against the tide.

There is a new taste on the wind,
A tang of sweet poison, tansy,
Perhaps, fresh mint, currency
Of freedom in progress.

Halfway
Looking to cast off with the sun
Rising clear and unveiled
And the breeze fair from the east,

The confines of the old port
Slip away – crowded moorings,
Safe havens, irrelevant refuge –
All obsolete.

* * *

Forgetting to pray in the bare temple,
Two children shriek, hide and seek
Each other among the whitened stones,
From hilltop to water,

Risk pebble-bruised feet to let the sea
Splash about their legs, gently tamper
With land clothes in the hidden cove,
Where only one boat rests at anchor,
Its single mast betraying, poking
Past the headland's barren rim.

* * *

I am so calm now.

* * *

The hills have powdered their faces
For Michaelmas: less than successful
Make-up. Old friends highlight
Crevices, drawing attention to their age.
I see them more often now and
Marvel at the viciousness
With which the sculptor
Uses his materials –
Ice, wind, rain,
Winter colours, rotten leaves, hollow eyes,
Lines, veins, leather.
Day after day old faithfuls drop
From lists and landscapes.

* * *

After two years, even less,
There are little signs of erosion,
An etch here, a gully scoured,
A certain settling of moraine into drumlins
Where my finger never used to deviate.

It takes one winter to tarnish glory.
After ten years the dereliction
Is past the help of machinery – more waste
From nature's wretched industry.
How cruel to let me meet you
That close to time's fulcrum
And watch you tip.

* * *

Most trees, young and old,
Are shaking off the tired fashions of summer
Perversely, like Cardiff girls,
Preferring to bare their tops
When the nights are coldest.
Some persevere with what they always wear
But look dowdy now,
Short needle hair, dark and brittle.
Come the spring these spinster regiments
Stay drab, approving only a touch
Of light relief when deciduous sisters
Explode in green – but that sister
Over there is wearing outrageous autumn colours.
I dread to think what she will choose for winter.

* * *

I am so calm now,
After the dreams have died.

* * *

But a remnant can still be detected
Under a layer of burned debris,

35

The rubble of destruction, traces of parkland,
Walls of one or two stone courses where once they rose
In turrets. Making out the floor plan,
The courtyards and fountains of the villa,
Can revive the shadow of that dream,
Send anticipation trickling through my veins.
I wonder whether to expose
These foundations to the air
Or bury them decently
For future generations to excavate.

* * *

A ruin is better left abandoned.

* * *

The fashion for renovation has had its day,
For taking a venerable skeleton,
Charming in her vernacular,
Improving the plumbing,
Slapping on some warm paint,
Ignoring the sagging plaster in obvious need
Of a buttress or two.
Restorers of thatch, of baize, cluck,
Shake heads in sympathy,
Deplore the enormity of the cost.
How can such dilapidation
Infect the fabric in less than thirty years,
Set in so relentlessly in four?

* * *

I'll wander off, leave the gate
Unlocked for casual thieves –

There's nothing interesting worth
Stealing now.

* * *

I have spent the night promising wonders,
Drawing on the energy of these decrepit streets,
The epic Manhattan
Grandeur of their corporate spires
Undermined nonchalantly,
Pimped by retail signage,
Careless, ugly come-ons.

* * *

Because a sudden beauty startled
The drab coffee-shop morning
Before she was forced to shed beguiling pink
For docile black, I could still celebrate
And wait for when wine, then music,
Elevated her again.

* * *

But that was long ago –
So long
It might even have been yesterday.

* * *

Today her eyes are in dark shadow
And her face has turned horsey,
No longer intriguing, only bitter, thin,
No longer enigmatic, only vapid,
All the hair limp, limbs unkempt,
Zest soured to acidic spit.

* * *

She had become my winter.
There were days when the light never showed,
When the only separation between nights
Was a veil of charcoal grey,
Barely worth pushing back the bedclothes for,
Without the energy even to rain,
Too sad for anger, too hopeless for resentment,
Senile, inhuman, loveless days.

* * *

They were enough to make Persephone restless.
She squirmed a little on the throne,
Shifting her pert and perfect bottom
In that tiresome way that told Hades
She would rather not be there,
That surely it must be time to rise again.

He sighed and gazed with sad tolerance
As his mistress, so young it was almost embarrassing
To be seen together outside his halls,
Smiled and glanced at the clock.
She looked just as good at night, he thought,
But daylight exposed his furrows with
Archaeological cruelty.

And so above snowdrops happened,
Tea was not always taken in the dark,
Adoration and discovery seemed possible once again,
With all the work that that implied,
And, in the foetal spring, desire
Could survive the frost of ridicule.

* * *

The snow teases, a duvet for the hills,
Then slips away, giggling in fluffy rivulets,
Rushing back at night to obliterate brown with white again,
Decorating the fringes,
The gullies and secret openings.
Demeter has bought some new lingerie
To cheer herself up in winter.

* * *

Such naughty innocence is dangerous.
There is no allowance for the wishes,
The paranoid desires of powerful men.
A force of nature, a goddess, is made to cry,
Her streams tearing down the cheeks of the hills,
Soaking the meadows into stagnant mud,
Her spirit almost as broken as her waters.
She has been pregnant with flowers for months now,
Sleeping through the brief days,
Working nights
To protect the princely buds in white tundra.
Birth is imminent, unstoppable,
Heads break through, wings stretch
Under splitting membrane, ready to unfurl.

* * *

What an affront to cold government,
To the official order conspiring to hold
Restless fecund earth under barren fetter.
This angel has no minister's permission,
No passport stamped and visaed,

Sanctioned by the old woman who has sold
Her own motherhood for the toys of inhuman power.
My goddess and her fledgling angel
Must reap poverty until politicians burn.

* * *

Another leaving
Across impatient seas
In the violent spring

* * *

I have found myself in a museum;
Or have I always lain there,
Itching to be found
Among the imprisoned art confined
To institutional walls washed magnolia
To reduce every image to banal
Anal equality? Across a landform
A child in a clear blue dress
Disports her freedom. She cannot
Read the notice, spot the cameras,
Know that she – her body,
Her laughter – is forbidden.

* * *

I need your voice to rise
Like lightning
From this stone

* * *

What sweet birth midnight brings;
As pain ebbs so begin the tears,
Carousing together in welcome and surprise.
Moments before, they shared a source.
Now, though, like mountains after
Earthquake, the reservoir has sundered.
Two springs, one birth in body split,
Erupting with the agony of joy.
You looked amazed at the brute
Business of welcome, the vicious
Colours, hard noise, noxious smells;
The shock would make a grown man cry,
But welcome you are and loved
In defiance of your conception.

* * *

If I were Ovid I could describe a nymph
Expelled a little way from her lush forest,
Lounging by a pool, garbed with unbecoming formality,
Staring in the direction of the sea.
She is so still she could be an elegant
Chameleon, people the flies.
Like all men I wait for the moment
When the nymph breaks her gaze from the water,
Forsakes the sea and lights on me.
It happens, swiftly, without remark,
A beam from a lighthouse circling dispassionately,
Bringing revelation. As a nymph,
Of course, she has no concern
For her effects on mortals.

* * *

Everything needs
To find a perfect place.

* * *

In the shallow pool beneath the nymph's gaze
An industrious little fish, not much more
Than a sprat, flicks her tail
Against the current of the rivulet.
She was there yesterday, braving the birds
In her sunlit water room,
Where the tasty insects puncture the roof.
All she needs is to dart
From weed wall to stick wall,
Fulfilling opportunities.
I can see her perfect place;
Mine is elusive still. I'll ask the nymph.
She will know the way, but will she tell?

* * *

Perhaps I shall park myself
In a place of literary notoriety,
Reminded, now, of the doggerel
I wrote for lost or imagined loves,
When every bar was a possible home,
Every home a probable prison.

Draw me in. Introduce me.
Give me a reason to regret
That the morning will bring postponement.

I want to believe that the gods
Have everything in hand – and
That before the northern night turns black
They will have made their move.

I will report.

* * *

The gods, as so often,
Had their minds
On other things.

* * *

I have journeyed for two days
Along unmade roads
To these fractured mountains, offering libations,
Watching the monotony of prayer,
Struck how despair has destroyed
Faith in simple tasks.
This country and this mountain share
Their metaphors – proud constructs
Left to weather as they will,
The certainty of rock shattered, allowed to tumble,
The winter detritus of fervent tumult.

* * *

I cannot tidy the buildings any more
Than the boulders from the scree.

* * *

43

Which discovery is more painful:
That love is divided
Or that the sundered parts,
Reassembled,
Do not make one mind, one body,
But are the spores in the herbaceous border,
Sprouting in unexpected places,
Anxious eyes by the roses,
Languid arms working their way
Up the garden seat, legs inverted,
Elegantly rising with fallen fruit
Ripening where they meet?
And across the whole curvaceous sweep
The riotous beauty of the wild display
Plays havoc with my future.

* * *

I am so calm now;
That is
Such sweet illusion.

* * *

Perhaps only in a tight Japanese garden,
Where the landscape is ordered far beyond nature,
Can water stand clear for very long.

Cherish that moment,
Before the wind ruffles,
Leaves fall, insects drown

And the stone bed becomes indistinct once again.

* * *

Arrows of desire
Do not converge,
But fly from horseback.
Some graze,
Some pierce exultantly.

* * *

Down in the mind's harbour,
My own Venetian lagoon,
My Serenissima, my darlings,
Replacements in the list for those tipped
Over time's fulcrum into the rubble,
Their exposed foundations
Having nothing left to steal,
My sudden beauties,
My soft wine and dark music,
For the spring, my luxuriant autumn,
Cashmere, my fledgling angels,

I long to sail among you,
Explore your alleys, laughing,
Ignore no-entry signs,
Penetrate your cul-de-sacs,
Scroll back and forth
Between
Between

* * *

Across the room, the street,
At the tram stop, another table,
Behind the counter, the bar,

45

Sudden beauty startles lazy desires
Into their accustomed frenzy,
Never mind the ridicule as they leap,
Ululate, rehearse their joy.

But the nymph's gaze returns to the water
Unimpressed, her brow furrowed
Against the interruption, the affront.

Only a little way behind her
All I can do
Is wave and smile in hope,
Translate the incoherent
Passion into music

And after scrolling round the world
Accosting dreams, look askance
At the discouragement her herald brings,
Signal this finish with a fanfare.

FINAL LOVER

If you arrive on Thursday and agree,
Become my final lover.
I will be fulfilled for all
These ebb-tide years, your prime.
Help me confound the puritans,
The damners, the fierce rule-setters.
Propel their disapproval into furthest space
Where our difference, our gold sliver of time,
Is just a gnat's flight across the sun.
There will be one more book of love songs.
Yours, if you arrive
On Thursday and agree.

WINTER TREACHERY

On the bare trees the apples still hang,
Shrivelled by this deep and early frost.
Pipes will puncture in their usual place,
Copper sliced by a scalpel of ice,
Winter's surgeon unwilling to wait
For the anaesthetic of lagging and heaters
To take the edge off this hidden pain.
On the back step the youngest cat
Gazes balefully at the locked door,
Willing it to open, allow the dart upstairs
To last week's warm bed, second-hand
Hot water bottle and the certainty of human care.
Only I know how callously such simple
Trust is broken.

SINGEL REVISITED

Generations of ginger cats have flicked
Their tails and slunk away since I first sat
At this window, letting trams interrupt
My reverie. They, trams and cats,
Are sleeker now, and I must change
My glasses if I am to read this page
And see if the Odeon sign still marks
The house across the bland canal.

I cannot remember who I loved
When I wrote at this table then,
Nor the second time, after twenty years,
In a lost poem, though I know
Who it should have been and rarely was.

Only the number and diversity of bikes
Propped against the wall and railings will alter
In the time it takes to come here again
And, with resignation realise, despite
The tumbling black glory of your hair,
Forbidden promise beneath loose cloth,
That you too have been forgotten.

LLANDIAN

A Response to London's Story

I

Late evening, late in the fifth month.

The tide rises with the moon and floods
From the dark river the little stream
That fringes Llud's gate, turning it from Fleet
And clear to brown and sullen,
Creeping over the edge of the westward road.

Up the hill in the temple girls chatter
As they prepare the night's offerings,
Keeping an eye out for their chief and the moment
When the pink edge of the clouds upriver
Resigns itself to twilight grey.

They watch too through the eastern colonnades.

Their mistress will rise full tonight.
Already she lurks bloated low on the skyline
As though her menstrual size so early
Will chase away the sun and force
The city gates to slam before their time.

She nurses herself for the perfect hour; the temple girls
Fidget more quietly now, impatient for the order
To carry the platters and lay them
On the trestles. Above, Diana, inhabiting her statue,
Waits for the moon to pierce fresh darkness
And give her life. She hunts
At night, and the offerings are those
Gathered for this moment in the week before.

New herbs, bluebells from the shady woods to the north,
Above all venison cut from a wounded stag
Who collapsed, a miracle, on the temple steps
In final supplication that auspicious morning.

The moon rose, the crystal eyes of the goddess
Flashed. Before her girls danced
As they ate the seasoned uncooked meat,
Propositioning each other's dreams.

II

Every afternoon ships dock against the quay
Below the makeshift bridge, creating
Competition for the ferry. Stevedores,
Freed men from wars in Egypt,
Illyria, Africa, hump the stores of oil,
Wine, hemp, precious plants to test the climate,
To the warehouses above the tideline.

There are cherry trees and vines,
Ornamental shrubs from high in Asia Minor,
Plums, too, but no hope
For olives in this rain and early frost.

Occasionally fighting animals, bears
And mountain lions so much more impressive
Than the native docile beasts (in a country
Where it is hard even to find a wolf)
Come ashore to spice the games,
Though the odds are always fixed – lions too valuable
For cheap slaves, condemned barbarians,
To be allowed to win.

Soldiers land away from the emergent city, downriver
At their spartan camps, and march briskly through
On their way to battles in the north and west.

From all across and up and down the island
Men converge to trade their treasures,
Copper and tin in fine-wrought bronze, gold,
Surplus women culled in vendettas
Too local for the world to care.

For seventy years the city grew, prospered,
Ignored the jealousies of lesser towns, the animosities
Aroused by armies it supplied, secretly despised.
Then news of unprecedented defeat
Sped south, a fetid wind, a tribe
They'd never heard of sought revenge for military rapes.

52

Boudicca, the terror queen, smashed the temple,
Slaughtered artists in the markets and left
Nothing but a layer of ash
To taunt imperial boasts.

III

The great dark river has dominion
In these few years when again only the wind,
The call of fractious birds, splash of otters,
Breaks the silence. From springs in low hills
Rivulets and becks, streams and tributaries,
Spill unsullied through virgin woods,
Cut their own free channels across marsh mud
At low tide, rush to join Tamesis on the high.

For a dozen seasons no humans name
Your spirits, distinguish between *afon*, *nant* and
Flumen, parade their filthy ships
On your natural waters, divert or dam you.

You can be yourselves, prick the land with ice
Or lie placid in the summer sun.

IV

Eventually the ash leached away or fed
Wild roses. A great wharf was built
And warehouses strung along the north bank.

Taverns opened between the counting house
Up to a noble forum resounding to merchant
Shouts from all across Rome's lands,
Selling must-have goods to pioneers and homesick,
Ambitious wives and Barbarian curious.

Diana's devotees returned and called on the moon
Again to bring fortune on the tide, make the roads
Safe enough for daily hunting. Other gods
Vied with her: Apollo, Minerva;
Neptune calling his sailors from wine shops
Back to sea.

Londinium would empty in years of plague
Or when the river stank
Like Tiber in the summer heat.
A city open to the world brought danger
As well as exotica, fleas and foreign rats
That tainted the perfumed baths, made
Brythonic girls wary of the charm
Of southern tongues.

In good years houses, villas, barbicans, brothels
Multiplied. In bad we sometimes felt like
Villagers in open fields between the temples.
When Diana was supplanted temples became
Churches, business failed, Rome forgot us,
Baths were filled with earth and not even
Arthur could make Londinium safe
From disease, neglect and Saxon spoil.

V

In the daytime forage in the brambles,
Graze a cow or two, let the pigs
Get drunk on rotting apples, once
In a while find an ancient jewel
To bauble rough cloth worn in timber huts.
At night, though, in fine spring evenings,
Dance among the fallen stones and wonder
Why those precarious columns
Point towards the moon.

VI

By the time the Confessor built his minster
In the west and the Conqueror his white
Tower at the eastern corner of the wall
Tranquil days and quiet nights were already
Five generations forgotten. Capital.
Capital noise, capital stench and ale,
Riot and regulation, thoroughfares
And fashion wares, prelates, prostitutes,
Aldermen and urchin pickpockets.
Houses crowd and crowds are housed,
Churches breed, rabbits have been banished.
Where Diana had held the hill, Paul was installed,
His temple burned, sacked, burned and burned again.
Free rivers found their names. Fleet and Tyburn,
Westbourne, Wandle, Lea and Walbrook
Shared Thames' tide and the names were bandied;

The streams tamed then, like all domestics,
Nonchalantly abused, ignored until they disappeared –
As if the river spirits who had flourished in the infant city
Could no longer protect even their physical form
Once the friars, black, white and grey,
Camped on their banks. With irony that history
Loves, the new river names attached themselves to churches
Of nothing saints, even as the waters
Were piped, blocked and over-paved.

Surely only the force of Diana's tide saved the dark river himself?
Though bridged and stuffed with dead and detritus,
He still bossed and sluiced his villages and city,
While from Tower to Thorney Isle palaces,
Castles, priories, Abbey defined the bank
(And even Lambeth's one dry plot), their gardens walled,
Shutting out the trade, traffic and turbulence beyond.

While kings pull archers from the fields
To ravage Celtic lands and lose their way
From Calais to Jerusalem, guilds grow rich,
Build their halls, adopt livery and impose
Rules stricter than the kings'.
The rest of us have fairs at Bart's and Southwark.
With the fairs come dancing, players, riot,
Football, music – so much music
Spilling from the buskers, the fruit and ribbon sellers,
Lovers with a gittern and a rebec slung from the shoulder,
Music leeching into the naves and taverns,
Raucous and refined, reverend and rude.

Such players all, even before the courtyards of the inns
Between the Winchester bishop's whorehouses
And the gatehouse of the bridge became our theatres;
Rose, Swan, George, enduring Globe, showing the tragedies
That tyrants bring, the comedy of suffering.
How else could playwrights write the truth
And keep their heads attached when one man's
Truth was another's sedition? If we survived
Suspicion, plague loved the summer stench,
Flu the winter ice and Lent brought famine
Without officious injunction from any priest.
Misfortune breeds envy, and envy puritans.
So they came and shut and smashed
And, when they got bored with black, plague
Returned until fire swept clean, charcoaled Paul's again.

In the moonlight that autumn Diana smiled,
Welcomed Cupid, sent him to the King
Promising better, greater times to come.

VII

Stand still and you will be swept away;
Stay silent and your language will shatter
As all the world shouts. Tides are everything:
Of traffic, bodies, money, water. In London
Fire cleans where rain stains. Palaces
Are tinder, theatres explode in fireworks,
Bankers have our fingers burned, coffee is roasted,
Gin fuels the fires within, cremates restraint.

Ovens, furnaces, forges, kilns, kitchens
Spew soot till it clouds the moon,
Renders pale Portland stone Edinburgh black.

From the moment when there was more money
In money than cows and land, this is the action city,
The screw and be screwed city.
Rule a short empire with a long reach,
Nothing is unsold, nothing without a price.
Be an urchin, pick a pocket or two,
Be an earl, evangelist,
Trader general and pick a country or two,
Create and dissipate, give two meanings
To exploit. Bank the river and the proceeds.

London sprawls and banks, river and profits,
Changes colour. A tinge of regret
Creeps in for pastoral pleasures lost.
A park the size of Monaco is saved from builders.
In Vauxhall and Marylebone Georgian beauties
Dance prettily and sing of Phyllis and Corydon,
Sweet Sylvia and Lysander, before Victorian
Railways sweep them away. Victoria
Rediscovers Highlands and Islands, London builds,
Erects a Crystal Palace for the world
And the world promenades and is impressed.

Watch then, as London burrows and bridges.
Thames no longer sprawls across Surrey,
But rushes between stone walls and stanchions,
His tides angry and full enough to carry

The greatest ships into dock, filling the old
Wastelands east of the Tower. What he has lost
In freedom he has gained in pride and power,
Filthy, killing his fish for the right
To battle Yangtze and Hudson for pre-eminence.
On either side of him the city digs. There are
Tunnels for shit and laundry water,
For people and post, cables and trains,
Rivers and munitions. As the lovers retire
To the country or hold ceremonies in suburbs,
Bridges multiply, and across them, in endless
Belching trains, the people of the new London,
The old villages, define new streams and tides.

The ring of stations, for carriages, not crosses,
Gorge commuters on the flow and ebb,
Send soldiers to slaughter, welcome Tchaikovsky,
Dvořák and Debussy off the boat train.
Dickensian grime becomes Elgarian Cockaigne
Until jealous Germany throngs the sky with bombs
And fire breaches Paul and Diana's temple once again.

VIII

After each destruction – Boudicca, Saxons,
Vikings, Black Death, Great Fire and Hitler –
Londoners paused…
For half a decade cleared bodies, rubble,
And installed a place for celebration;
After Boudicca, the amphitheatre,

After Hitler, the Festival Hall.
Again the world arrived, rushed:
First on ships from colonies, dominions,
Then through skies and one great tunnel
Till the rhythms and dances of London
Did not echo the globe, they sent it spinning,
Leaping, warming on a tide of rising
Song and glass, capturing the sun.

Keep rabid puritans at bay – those
Who always disapprove, sanction a bomb
To make a deadly irrelevant point.
Instead give us free spirits, mixers, blend
Our skins and recipes, let limbs entwine in love.

Shall we free our rivers now, garden their banks,
And, as lights embolden the night,
Raise wine, Llandian's long libation to the moon?

ANGEL MATCH

Fallen vs. Unfallen

Facing defeat, three–nil,
Losing by a trinity, the Angels
Change tactics, forget
Clever nutmegs, subtle practice.
Time for the long ball, the strong ball,
Wrong ball in the box,
Fox the Devils, the rebels,
Wing backs hurling forward,
Wings unleashed, unfurled,
Passing wide, cross wing
To wing, cross to the D,
Strike first touch,
Volley straight in, avenge,
Goal, GOAL, GOOOOOOAAAAAALL!

Haloes up now, Angels surge,
Devil shoots wide, slides
Into a tackle. Red Devil, red card,
Penalty, missed wide? No!
Three–two; final minute,
Last attack; who dares
Rule an Angel offside?
Three–three; heavenly honour
Saved. Virtue complete.

61

MATCH REPORT

In heaven it is hard to criticise,
But there were long-term residents
Who came close and ventured a suggestion
That you didn't need to be a prophet
To predict there would be problems
When the Fit Angels played the Hades Allstars
In a one-off reconciliation match.

For convenient viewing the top authorities
Decreed the Elysian Fields the perfect venue
To grumbles from below – very difficult
For Hades supporters to attend,
And too much home advantage
(The fallen angels trained on a cinder pitch,
Not this manicured velvet lawn,
Mown and watered, brushed and buffed immaculate
By saints with time on their hands).

The choice of referee caused consternation.
He/she couldn't be a devil, obviously –
No trust there – but to be fair, an angel neither.
Eventually, reluctantly, the authorities plumped
For a deity of an external persuasion.

With solemn grins, never able to resist temptation,
The Universal Council nominated an elephant god
Quite unable to keep up with the game, assisted
By a pair of satyrs, flags gripped in tails,
Trotting along the touchlines.
Nobody wanted the pink and orange ball.

From the first trumpet to the last
The accusations flew as fast
As the fouls, the tackles, the ankle nips,
The tweaked feathers and tugged horns.

There was trouble down wings and with wings,
Black poking in angelic eyes,
White furling round devilish bodies
In the six yard box, giving the goalkeeper
No view at all at corners, at free kicks,
Spreading to unfair advantage in the wall.

The ref missed a wing ball in the area –
Certain penalty, not given, but not forgotten.
Two Hades backs lost their tempers,
Again, could not cool down.
One was shown a straight red.

In the fracas that followed
No Allstar noticed the third Angel substitute,
A cherub, slip on, shimmy, tuck
The ball low into the corner of their net.
It's tough at the bottom.
Full time: Angels 3–Allstars 2.
No rematch for aeons.

SEVEN POEMS

FOR BLOOD ORANGE'S EXHIBITION

IN BRUSSELS

1. THE ICE BELL
Artist: Aaron McPeake

You were cast as solidly
As your brass brothers,
Yet while you wait
For the strike of passing hands,
The violence that makes them sing,
You drip soundlessly to nothing.
Da capo.

2. DISTURBANCES
Artist: Blue Firth

You cannot disturb me –
I am immune, so analogue,
Locked happily in real time,
Fortified against app and iPhone,
Headphone, web location, your switch.
Whisper this for me instead –
Is love infectious?

3. CATENARY WALL
Artist: George Eksts

Too neat for a beach, too flimsy
For a hammock, each nodule
Riveted with care, prolonged
Beyond function, uneasy conceits.
But I wanted shells and water
And a reflection of my own
Cruel litter, abandoned wheat.

4. NON-STOP EVOLUTION
Artist: Madalina Zaharia

We demand progress, insist
That the past is just that,
A curiosity without context.
Most of the time, wasted time,
We just run rings around ourselves.

5. AJPART
Artist: Peter Downsbrough

Now they've put the cars in prison,
Backs against the bars, the only view
Each other's darkened headlights.
There are so many mirrors to see
The world outside. Why look, though?
A glimpse will not trigger their release.
It will rain soon, it always does.

6. UNTITLED
(A woman's stone head with phones, no body)
Artist: Michael van den Abeele

There is only your head left, and the phones
To shut in stray thoughts. The shoulder
That I kissed on our first morning
Has gone, its scent of lemon squandered.
Only imaginary music remains: a little Cage.
Perhaps I can summon some Mahler
To resurrect and spring awaken.

7. FISH
Artist: Shelley Nadashi

However hard these fish swim against
The white tide, however they flick
Tails at us, the wall, the dry air,
A fish can never escape a frame
Any more than I can break (so stern)
Your terms and my condition,
Resolute fish, confines forever strict.

NIGHT TRAIN

FROM ULAANBAATAR

The train shrieks as it leaves UB,
Knows pain in the bones beneath its sleepers
As it rolls out across the desert
Or drags itself north,
Hills and wretched plains
Fierce until the Urals.

To the Western ear, that elongated
Plaintive hoot could hardly be more redolent;
Formidable distance, exotic abandonment
Of normal time, its romance almost
As unspoilt as the careless landscape,
It tries to cheer either side of this gruff city.

Still, it carries politics with every pull,
Sometimes people, sometimes mountain guts,
Ripped wholesale to glut factories
Ravenous for merchants' rock.
Cross either border, relinquish freedom
And the horses flee.

INTERLUDE

Wait, attention, watch out,
Much the same in garbled French,
Conveying the desperation
Of wasted time, the coffees and the wine,
The scrutiny of strangers, the smoke,
The tired desires, the futile smiles.
Between the games I am empty.
So few of us are young enough,
Or beautiful, to bring on the songs.
Attending my non-appointment
I dare the words to presage hope,
Attend, attente, entend, entente...

VENETIAN SERENADE

Venice, c.1730. The scene is a small piazza which has one side facing the water of the Grand Canal on the opposite side, but close to San Marco. At one side is a small chapel with its door half open. The last purchasers of the day are examining the trinkets on the hawkers' stalls. A woman, the singer, enters cautiously, ignores the stalls, peers into but doesn't enter the chapel, then goes to look out across the lagoon.

PRELUDE
(instrumental)

MOVEMENT I
Andante – subito adagio – andante

(recit)
I arrive for him early, while the sun
Still shoots late spring darts across the water,
Hawkers sell their tourist junk without enthusiasm –
They have languished at their stalls
While other men siesta. Every purchase of glass,
A bauble, a hook-nosed mask, a pottery saint,
Requires the energy for a forced smile,
A tilt back of the hat.

Cats begin to stir for the evening's hunting.
We have picked the place carefully,
Well away from Rialto and across
From the great palazzi. The trade
Of gallants, courtesans and spies
Thins like the canals themselves,
Becomes alley shifty, lurking for opportunity.

The little piazza we have chosen is open
But secluded, half of one side viewing the lagoon.
I can lean against a parapet,
Watch the boats undisturbed,
Unsolicited by priests or worse.

(aria)

In this light,
This late day's glow,
I bask, bask in the late sun,
Anticipate with joy, alive
To Venezia, Venezia,
Great haven, water jewel
Of the south – as am I!
An amulet drifting on the gentle tide.

(recit)

Behind me a solid door stands ajar,
A small sanctuary for retreat,
Revelation or assignation.

The water darkens and on landing steps
Men lift torches into brackets as the sun dips,
Bored strollers sigh, sidle
Over to me in hope of favours. I disdain them.
The women assess me for competition,
A faint wind ruffles the flames and tosses clean air
Along the dank canals, freshening the piazza.

Bells peel for vespers. The doors of the chapel
Are thrown open and the priest ushers me to join
Him inside. This too I decline. Hawkers pack
Their stalls, glance at me, hoping I might be
The answer to their evening prayers.
I turn away; they shrug but are not discouraged.
I must resist them, sure that my love will appear soon.

(aria)

Am I right? Right to wait
So late here,
Right here, not late,
My state still light,
Right hour, our own piazza.
I shall, shall not fight
My desire, the evening fire.

(faster)

Early, too early, I pace,
Trace the water, the chancers,
Glancers, fresh dancers,
Finger free, facing, chasing me.

DANCE

II
Largo

(*recit*)

I count the strokes of the bells and settle,
Content, watching the shadows, searching
For more than a cat, less than the curiosity of strangers.
Solitary bells strike quarters, never in agreement.
Beyond San Marco, from beneath the shallows,
The moon creeps into the silent sky.
Below me placid waves lap against stone.

The cats grow bold. I hold my station,
Shy of all attention, dreaming of the hours to come.
I lean and count the degrees, moon to water,
Woman to man, stone to shadow, repeating
Paces, glances, guesses about entrances,
Your arrival, my reaction. Time slows.
Solitary time and the perfect symmetry of
Anticipated dreams hold the city in my thrall.

DANCE

III
Agitato

(*recit*)

That clock, that strike, no calming bell,
An alarm, strident, cracking the moon,
Hurling white horses against my coast,

72

My island rock, scratching at indecent fears.
So dark now, and only one torch in the far corner
Breaks it, flickering shadows more frightful
Than the steady block of the unlit doorways.

(*aria*)

Everywhere shadows,
Never still in the torchlight,
Foretelling ruin. Look, even
My trembling hands play the game,
Flicking trails of black flame
Against the wall,
Bringing stones to violent life.

I am alone, surrounded by these
Taunting shadows. Only the brightest moon
Or my tardy lover can deliver me.

My lover – long for the reach
Of his fingers, searching
Like the shadows, touching,
Asking for all I can give. I will,
I can, I shall.

(*recit*)

Nothing, no one, comes to meet me.
He's not coming, I know that now.
There has been no accident, just betrayal,
And his laughter at my waiting, my danger.
At the next quarter I will go.
Pray for me in these streets.

DANCE

IV
Allegro – Adagio

(*recit*)

Behind me the moon is rising,
Reaching towards me from Istria.
At first only the lagoon and
Gondolas are caught. I can see the boats
Without lanterns lolling at their moorings.
Soon the parapet is breached. The piazza
Has shape and edges once again.
I really am alone, without lover
But without threat, no lunges
From cold undiscovered hands.

I have worn my grey cloak dusted with Murano glass.
In the shadows I will see him before he knows me,
But in the moonlight, the high brazen moonlight,
I am a silver beacon, a living ghost of Diana,
Sentry on guard before the blackened sanctuary,
Impatient, irresolute, restless
As the night's fresh and sniping wind.

(*aria*)

Why, why risk my reputation,
My safety, my name, my body,
Let men mistake me for a whore,
Let whores mistake me for them?

The law of love gives me courage,
Sets out the rewards for patience.
I shiver, now with fear,
Soon with pleasure.

V

Coda

(*recit*)

The bells strike once more and I rustle my cloak to leave.
Then, breaking from the shadow street, he rushes,
Turning to flash his sword back into the resistant night.
He stops before me, disarms, pushes the silver canopy
From my hair and, as silent as the moon, guides
Me to our temple for our tale of captured hearts.

DANCE

(*aria*)

At last his arms protect.
We can dance, chance the moon,
Charm the lagoon,
Release my heart.

75

EPILOGUE I

By the sea I mourn
The blue sea turning grey,
Shore's rocks laid bare by
Age and tempest, stripped of life,
No pickings for the gulls,
The cloud bloated with rain,
Molluscs struggling
For purchase in the storm.

I mourn the inconclusions,
Love's cliffs reduced to pebbles,
Passions dwindling to inconsequence.
I mourn that beauty is out of reach,
My search for it derided, abhorred.

To love a caricature
Is all that is allowed, a ghoul,
Tattered remnant of womanhood,
Just as I am of the man
Whose smiles taunt me from the kitchen wall.

VICTORIAN WALTZ

She cascaded in time with him,
Her face alive, shoulders rolling,
Feet as often off the floor
As her dress, his strong hands,
Would let them lift.
Counting, she wheeled,
One-two-three,
One-two-three,
One-two-three,
Squeeze, spin, skip,
Nothing tempered, nothing contained.
She called for another, demanded freedom,
More dance, more music, more speed;
Refused to believe
This sudden love
Was nothing greater
Than heat, noise and
Too much punch.

POSTSCRIPT

The title of this book was chosen several years before its publication in 2021, but the complications and restrictions of the COVID-19 period have made it even more apt. The travels in Italy and Greece, the Balkans and Chile, even Brussels and Paris, which it chronicles have become the stuff of dreams and impractical longings, no longer the norm for an itinerant writer. In 2019 I visited over a dozen countries around Europe and as far south as Tanzania. As I write this, I have been confined to Caithness in the far north of Scotland, mostly alone, for sixteen months: good for routine writing, bad for inspiration and sanity.

Music, electronically provided, has become even more essential than normal, but the rituals of live music-making, the companionship of musicians at concerts, the chance to get lost in the glorious acoustic wash of sound and then chew over the experience around a table afterwards, have all but disappeared. Festivals, those joyous concentrations where you can lurch from hall to hall with barely enough time for a sandwich in between, have all either been postponed or confined to screens. Personally I hate concerts on screen. It is impossible to focus, and directors rarely pick the right view. Perhaps because of all that, the projects and relationships that gave rise to many of these poems have become even more precious.

In the mean time, the position of all the arts has become more precarious. Politics, mainly tawdry right wing, but also from the puritanical left, have intervened at almost every level in Britain to the detriment of students, freelance professionals, orchestras, broadcasters and producers. If this was the early nineteenth century I would be on Hazlitt's side in bemoaning the philistinism and small-mindedness of contemporary politicians. The only hope is that ours will be forgotten or redundant in a decade or two. Around the world standards of official behaviour are not just slipping, they are cascading to fresh lows of autocracy, irresponsibility and shamelessness; a pessimistic sign that humanity has not moved away as far as it should from the rubbish of previous centuries. The need for co-operation in the face of natural crisis is at the mercy of venality and short-term convenience. Perhaps it always was. It is still worse than unattractive.

That is all too depressing, though. I hope those that are now children will be able to read these words when they are my age with an indulgent smile, in the knowledge that the first half of the twenty-first century was not a complete waste of effort, and that these poems from its second decade celebrate as much as they mourn. The ideals of love, whether for a person or a landscape, a remnant of the past or the sudden glory of good music, are never out of date.

SIMON MUNDY
Summer 2021

SIMON MUNDY studied drama at university, but soon veered towards writing poetry and reviews, and at 23 he found himself a music critic and arts journalist. A champion of the arts, he has served as Director of the National Campaign for the Arts and Vice-President of PEN International's Writers for Peace Committee, and he co-founded the European Forum for the Arts and Heritage; he remains an adviser to the European Festivals Association. His writing includes biographies, novels, non-fiction, playscripts and poetry. *Waiting for Music* is his fifth poetry collection. For the last forty years Simon has bounced between Mid Wales, the far north of Scotland, London and Brussels. He likes his indecision.

More poetry by Simon Mundy:

Letter to Carolina
By Fax to Alice Springs
After the Games
More for Helen of Troy